Great Works Instructional Guides for Literature

The Great Gatsby

D1733788

A guide for the novel by F. Scott Fitzgerald
Great Works Author: Shelly Buchanan

SHELL EDUCATION

Publishing Credits

Jill K. Mulhall, Editor

Image Credits

Shutterstock (cover)

Standards

© 2007 Teachers of English to Speakers of Other Languages, Inc. (TESOL)
© 2007 Board of Regents of the University of Wisconsin System. World-Class Instructional Design and Assessment (WIDA)
© Copyright 2010. National Governors Association Center for Best Practices and Council of Chief State School Officers.
All rights reserved.

Shell Education

5301 Oceanus Drive
Huntington Beach, CA 92649-1030
http://www.shelleducation.com

ISBN 978-1-4258-8993-7
© 2015 Shell Educational Publishing, Inc.

Printed in USA. WOR004

The classroom teacher may reproduce copies of materials in this book for classroom use only. The reproduction of any part for an entire school or school system is strictly prohibited. No part of this publication may be transmitted, stored, or recorded in any form without written permission from the publisher.

Table of Contents

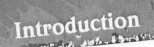

How to Use This Literature Guide

Today's standards demand rigor and relevance in the reading of complex texts. The units in this series guide teachers in a rich and deep exploration of worthwhile works of literature for classroom study. The most rigorous instruction can also be interesting and engaging!

Many current strategies for effective literacy instruction have been incorporated into these instructional guides for literature. Throughout the units, text-dependent questions are used to determine comprehension of the book as well as student interpretation of the vocabulary words. The books chosen for the series are complex exemplars of carefully crafted works of literature. Close reading is used throughout the units to guide students toward revisiting the text and using textual evidence to respond to prompts orally and in writing. Students must analyze the story elements in multiple assignments for each section of the book. All of these strategies work together to rigorously guide students through their study of literature.

The next few pages will make clear how to use this guide for a purposeful and meaningful literature study. Each section of this guide is set up in the same way to make it easier for you to implement the instruction in your classroom.

Theme Thoughts

The great works of literature used throughout this series have important themes that have been relevant to people for many years. Many of the themes will be discussed during the various sections of this instructional guide. However, it would also benefit students to have independent time to think about the key themes of the novel.

Before students begin reading, have them complete *Pre-Reading Theme Thoughts* (page 13). This graphic organizer will allow students to think about the themes outside the context of the story. They'll have the opportunity to evaluate statements based on important themes and defend their opinions. Be sure to have students keep their papers for comparison to the *Post-Reading Theme Thoughts* (page 64). This graphic organizer is similar to the pre-reading activity. However, this time, students will be answering the questions from the point of view of one of the characters of the novel. They have to think about how the character would feel about each statement and defend their thoughts. To conclude the activity, have students compare what they thought about the themes before they read the novel to what the characters discovered during the story.

How to Use This Literature Guide (cont.)

Vocabulary

Each teacher overview page has definitions and sentences about how key vocabulary words are used in the section. These words should be introduced and discussed with students. There are two student vocabulary activity pages in each section. On the first page, students are asked to define the ten words chosen by the author of this unit. On the second page in most sections, each student will select at least eight words that he or she finds interesting or difficult. For each section, choose one of these pages for your students to complete. With either assignment, you may want to have students get into pairs to discuss the meanings of the words. Allow students to use reference guides to define the words. Monitor students to make sure the definitions they have found are accurate and relate to how the words are used in the text.

On some of the vocabulary student pages, students are asked to answer text-related questions about the vocabulary words. The following question stems will help you create your own vocabulary questions if you'd like to extend the discussion.

- How does this word describe _____'s character?
- In what ways does this word relate to the problem in this story?
- How does this word help you understand the setting?
- In what ways is this word related to the story's solution?
- Describe how this word supports the novel's theme of . . . .
- What visual images does this word bring to your mind?
- For what reasons might the author have chosen to use this particular word?

At times, more work with the words will help students understand their meanings. The following quick vocabulary activities are a good way to further study the words.

- Have students practice their vocabulary and writing skills by creating sentences and/or paragraphs in which multiple vocabulary words are used correctly and with evidence of understanding.
- Students can play vocabulary concentration. Students make a set of cards with the words and a separate set of cards with the definitions. Then, students lay the cards out on the table and play concentration. The goal of the game is to match vocabulary words with their definitions.
- Students can create word journal entries about the words. Students choose words they think are important and then describe why they think each word is important within the novel.

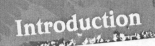

How to Use This Literature Guide *(cont.)*

Analyzing the Literature

After students have read each section, hold small-group or whole-class discussions. Questions are written at two levels of complexity to allow you to decide which questions best meet the needs of your students. The Level 1 questions are typically less abstract than the Level 2 questions. Level 1 is indicated by a square, while Level 2 is indicated by a triangle. These questions focus on the various story elements, such as character, setting, and plot. Student pages are provided if you want to assign these questions for individual student work before your group discussion. Be sure to add further questions as your students discuss what they've read. For each question, a few key points are provided for your reference as you discuss the novel with students.

Reader Response

In today's classrooms, there are often great readers who are below average writers. So much time and energy is spent in classrooms getting students to read on grade level, that little time is left to focus on writing skills. To help teachers include more writing in their daily literacy instruction, each section of this guide has a literature-based reader response prompt. Each of the three genres of writing is used in the reader responses within this guide: narrative, informative/explanatory, and argument. Students have a choice between two prompts for each reader response. One response requires students to make connections between the reading and their own lives. The other prompt requires students to determine text-to-text connections or connections within the text.

Close Reading the Literature

Within each section, students are asked to closely reread a short section of text. Since some versions of the novels have different page numbers, the selections are described by chapter and location, along with quotations to guide the readers. After each close reading, there are text-dependent questions to be answered by students.

Encourage students to read each question one at a time and then go back to the text and discover the answer. Work with students to ensure that they use the text to determine their answers rather than making unsupported inferences. Once students have answered the questions, discuss what they discovered. Suggested answers are provided in the answer key.

How to Use This Literature Guide (cont.)

Close Reading the Literature (cont.)

The generic, open-ended stems below can be used to write your own text-dependent questions if you would like to give students more practice.

- Give evidence from the text to support . . . .
- Justify your thinking using text evidence about . . . .
- Find evidence to support your conclusions about . . . .
- What text evidence helps the reader understand . . . ?
- Use the book to tell why _____ happens.
- Based on events in the story, ...
- Use text evidence to describe why . . . .

Making Connections

The activities in this section help students make cross-curricular connections to writing, mathematics, science, social studies, or the fine arts. Each of these types of activities requires higher-order thinking skills from students.

Creating with the Story Elements

It is important to spend time discussing the common story elements in literature. Understanding the characters, setting, and plot can increase students' comprehension and appreciation of the story. If teachers discuss these elements daily, students will more likely internalize the concepts and look for the elements in their independent reading. Another important reason for focusing on the story elements is that students will be better writers if they think about how the stories they read are constructed.

Students are given three options for working with the story elements. They are asked to create something related to the characters, setting, or plot of the novel. Students are given a choice on this activity so that they can decide to complete the activity that most appeals to them. Different multiple intelligences are used so that the activities are diverse and interesting to all students.

How to Use This Literature Guide (cont.)

Culminating Activity

This open-ended, cross-curricular activity requires higher-order thinking and allows for a creative product. Students will enjoy getting the chance to share what they have discovered through reading the novel. Be sure to allow them enough time to complete the activity at school or home.

Comprehension Assessment

The questions in this section are modeled after current standardized tests to help students analyze what they've read and prepare for tests they may see in their classrooms. The questions are dependent on the text and require critical-thinking skills to answer.

Response to Literature

The final post-reading activity is an essay based on the text that also requires further research by students. This is a great way to extend this book into other curricular areas. A suggested rubric is provided for teacher reference.

Correlation to the Standards

Shell Education is committed to producing educational materials that are research and standards based. As part of this effort, we have correlated all of our products to the academic standards of all 50 states, the District of Columbia, the Department of Defense Dependents Schools, and all Canadian provinces.

Purpose and Intent of Standards

Standards are designed to focus instruction and guide adoption of curricula. Standards are statements that describe the criteria necessary for students to meet specific academic goals. They define the knowledge, skills, and content students should acquire at each level. Standards are also used to develop standardized tests to evaluate students' academic progress. Teachers are required to demonstrate how their lessons meet standards. Standards are used in the development of all of our products, so educators can be assured they meet high academic standards.

How to Find Standards Correlations

To print a customized correlation report of this product for your state, visit our website at http://www.shelleducation.com and follow the online directions. If you require assistance in printing correlation reports, please contact our Customer Service Department at 1-877-777-3450.

Correlation to the Standards (cont.)

Standards Correlation Chart

The lessons in this guide were written to support the Common Core College and Career Readiness Anchor Standards. This chart indicates which sections of this guide address the anchor standards.

Common Core College and Career Readiness Anchor Standard	Section
CCSS.ELA-Literacy.CCRA.R.1—Read closely to determine what the text says explicitly and to make logical inferences from it; cite specific textual evidence when writing or speaking to support conclusions drawn from the text.	Analyzing the Literature Sections 1–5; Close Reading the Literature Sections 1–5; Making Connections Sections 1–2; Creating with the Story Elements Sections 1–5; Culminating Activity
CCSS.ELA-Literacy.CCRA.R.2—Determine central ideas or themes of a text and analyze their development; summarize the key supporting details and ideas.	Analyzing the Literature Sections 1–5; Making Connections Sections 1–4; Culminating Activity; Post-Reading Response to Literature
CCSS.ELA-Literacy.CCRA.R.3—Analyze how and why individuals, events, or ideas develop and interact over the course of a text.	Analyzing the Literature Sections 1–5; Close Reading the Literature Sections 1–5; Creating with the Story Elements Sections 1–5; Culminating Activity; Post-Reading Response to Literature
CCSS.ELA-Literacy.CCRA.R.4—Interpret words and phrases as they are used in a text, including determining technical, connotative, and figurative meanings, and analyze how specific word choices shape meaning or tone.	Vocabulary Sections 1–5; Analyzing the Literature Sections 1–5; Making Connections Section 2
CCSS.ELA-Literacy.CCRA.R.6—Assess how point of view or purpose shapes the content and style of a text.	Creating with the Story Elements Sections 1–5; Culminating Activity; Post-Reading Theme Thoughts
CCSS.ELA-Literacy.CCRA.R.8—Delineate and evaluate the argument and specific claims in a text, including the validity of the reasoning as well as the relevance and sufficiency of the evidence.	Making Connections Section 2; Post-Reading Response to Literature
CCSS.ELA-Literacy.CCRA.W.1—Write arguments to support claims in an analysis of substantive topics or texts using valid reasoning and relevant and sufficient evidence.	Reader Response Sections 2–3, 5; Making Connections Section 3; Post-Reading Response to Literature
CCSS.ELA-Literacy.CCRA.W.2—Write informative/explanatory texts to examine and convey complex ideas and information clearly and accurately through the effective selection, organization, and analysis of content.	Reader Response Sections 1, 3–5; Making Connections Section 5; Post-Reading Response to Literature
CCSS.ELA-Literacy.CCRA.W.3—Write narratives to develop real or imagined experiences or events using effective technique, well-chosen details and well-structured event sequences.	Creating with the Story Elements Sections 1–5; Reader Response Sections 1–2, 4
CCSS.ELA-Literacy.CCRA.W.4—Produce clear and coherent writing in which the development, organization, and style are appropriate to task, purpose, and audience.	Creating with the Story Elements Sections 1–5; Reader Response Sections 1–5; Making Connections Section 3; Post-Reading Response to Literature

Correlation to the Standards (cont.)

Standards Correlation Chart (cont.)

Common Core College and Career Readiness Anchor Standard	Section
CCSS.ELA-Literacy.CCRA.W.6—Use technology, including the Internet, to produce and publish writing and to interact and collaborate with others.	Making Connections Section 4; Creating with the Story Elements Sections 2–5
CCSS.ELA-Literacy.CCRA.W.9—Draw evidence from literary or informational texts to support analysis, reflection, and research.	Reader Response Sections 1–5; Close Reading the Literature Sections 1–5; Making Connections Section 5; Culminating Activity; Post-Reading Response to Literature
CCSS.ELA-Literacy.CCRA.L.1—Demonstrate command of the conventions of standard English grammar and usage when writing or speaking.	Reader Response Sections 1–5; Close Reading the Literature Sections 1–5; Making Connections Section 5; Culminating Activity; Post-Reading Response to Literature
CCSS.ELA-Literacy.CCRA.L.4—Determine or clarify the meaning of unknown and multiple-meaning words and phrases by using context clues, analyzing meaningful word parts, and consulting general and specialized reference materials, as appropriate.	Vocabulary Sections 1–5
CCSS.ELA-Literacy.CCRA.L.6—Acquire and use accurately a range of general academic and domain-specific words and phrases sufficient for reading, writing, speaking, and listening at the college and career readiness level; demonstrate independence in gathering vocabulary knowledge when encountering an unknown term important to comprehension or expression.	Vocabulary Sections 1–5

TESOL and WIDA Standards

The lessons in this book promote English language development for English language learners. The following TESOL and WIDA English Language Development Standards are addressed through the activities in this book:

- **Standard 1:** English language learners communicate for social and instructional purposes within the school setting.

- **Standard 2:** English language learners communicate information, ideas and concepts necessary for academic success in the content area of language arts.

About the Author—F. Scott Fitzgerald

F. Scott Fitzgerald is considered by many to be the greatest American novelist. Fitzgerald was born on September 24, 1896, in St. Paul, Minnesota. He was named after Francis Scott Key, a distant cousin. Fitzgerald was a writer from a very early age; his first published piece appeared in his grade school newspaper when he was 13. While writing for several school publications and the university theater program at Princeton, his studies took a back seat. He was forced to drop out in his third year due to poor academic performance. Fitzgerald joined the army and was stationed in the South. In Alabama he met the love of his life, Zelda Sayre, who at first rebuffed his advances due to his lack of prestige and financial success. Motivated to win Zelda's heart, Fitzgerald left Alabama for New York City, where he joined an advertising firm, hoping to launch a lucrative career. However, he couldn't resist a return to writing. He quit his job and moved back to St. Paul to rewrite an earlier, unsuccessful novel. It was soon published to critical acclaim and record sales as *This Side of Paradise*. A week after this novel's glowing reception, Zelda and Scott were married.

Following Fitzgerald's huge financial and popular success, Zelda and he embarked on a life of parties and extravagance. To fund this lifestyle, Fitzgerald wrote short stories for popular magazines like the *Saturday Evening Post* and *Esquire*. This path lost him much of his literary reputation and cachet during his lifetime, as some critics viewed him as a shallow playboy and a hack writer with little dedication. However, during this time Fitzgerald diligently chronicled the culture of the day, detailing the wealth, excesses, art, and ambitions of the 1920s. He dubbed the era the "Jazz Age," and this name has stood the test of time in both academic and popular history books.

Looking for a change of scenery and some fresh writing inspiration, the Fitzgeralds traveled to France in 1924 and stayed for a year. It was in Valescure that Fitzgerald penned his finest novel and one of America's defining stories. Published in 1925, *The Great Gatsby* depicts the Jazz Age, with all its materialism, excess, and distortion of the American Dream. It was not well received when first published, nor ever in Fitzgerald's lifetime, but it did gain high praise and admiration by literary scholars and critics by the 1950s and 1960s.

After the publication of *The Great Gatsby*, Fitzgerald's life took a downward turn. Always a heavy drinker as an adult, Fitzgerald's alcoholism wreaked havoc on his health. His wife Zelda succumbed to schizophrenia. In an attempt to revive his writing career, Fitzgerald moved to Hollywood, where he enjoyed mild success as a screenwriter and freelance storywriter. He died in 1940 at the age of 44, feeling he had been a failure as a writer despite being responsible for more than 170 publications. Since his death, Fitzgerald's reputation has skyrocketed. *The Great Gatsby* remains required reading in many high schools and colleges and continues to transport readers to an important time in American history. Many people consider it to be the greatest American novel.

Possible Texts for Text Comparisons

F. Scott Fitzgerald's other novels include *This Side of Paradise*, *Tender Is the Night*, and *The Beautiful and the Damned*. Some of his most famous short stories are "The Diamond as Big as the Ritz," "The Curious Case of Benjamin Button," "The Camel's Back," "The Last of the Belles," and the collection *Tales of the Jazz Age: 11 Classic Short Stories*.

Book Summary of *The Great Gatsby*

Nick Carraway narrates this story of a doomed love triangle between Jay Gatsby, Daisy Buchanan and her husband, Tom Buchanan. Nick becomes involved soon after he arrives in West Egg, a wealthy neighborhood inhabited by the newly rich. Upon his arrival, Nick pays a visit to his cousin Daisy, who lives across the water in East Egg, the older, more prestigious community founded by the established rich. Daisy's wealthy and controlling husband Tom is an old college friend of Nick's. Nick also meets Jordan Baker, an enigmatic and attractive friend of Daisy's.

Nick soon learns that the humble home he is renting in West Egg is right next door to the home of the prominent figure Jay Gatsby, who is known for his lavish summer parties. He meets the enigmatic Gatsby at one such party. In the meantime, Nick learns that Tom, a known philanderer, is having an indiscreet affair with Myrtle Wilson, a gaudy middle-class socialite.

Later, when in New York City with Gatsby, Nick learns more of his neighbor's story. It turns out that Gatsby met Daisy several years earlier and fell hopelessly in love with her. In pursuit of her, he earned his fortune and bought the huge mansion across the sound from the Buchanan home, hoping to attract Daisy's attention and admiration. Nick and Jordan Baker conspire to bring Gatsby and Daisy together. They succeed in reviving the relationship between the one-time lovers.

Gatsby and Daisy's relationship heats up. One hot afternoon, Nick, Jordan, Daisy, Tom, and Gatsby all go together to the Plaza Hotel in New York City. Tom sees the romantic relationship made apparent by Gatsby and Daisy. Enraged, he orders the party over and sends the two back to East Egg together. On the drive home, Daisy hits and kills Myrtle Wilson, Tom's lover, while driving Gatsby's car. Gatsby takes the blame. The following day, Myrtle's husband goes hunting for Myrtle's killer. He shoots and kills Gatsby, then himself.

Nick finds that no one seems to care about Gatsby's death. He is left to organize the funeral, which is attended by only a few. Disgusted with the shallow ideals and violent behavior he has witnessed, Nick decides to return home to the Midwest. The story ends after Nick and Tom see each other one last time and Nick fully realizes how careless Tom and those of his class truly are. Nick stands at the end of Gatsby's dock looking out across the water, contemplating all that happened.

Cross-Curricular Connection

The pursuit of the American Dream and the idea that any citizen, no matter how poor and disenfranchised, can live the rags to riches story is one still held and valued by many today.

Possible Texts for Text Sets

- Hemingway, Ernest. *In Our Time*. Scribner, 2003.
- Porter, Katherine Anne. *Ship of Fools*. Back Bay Books, 1984.
- Waugh, Evelyn. *Brideshead Revisited*. Back Bay Books, 2012.
- Wharton, Edith. *The House of Mirth*. Virago UK, 2006.
- Wilde, Oscar. *The Picture of Dorian Gray*. Spear Press, 2013.

Name _____

Date _____

Pre-Reading Theme Thoughts

Directions: Read each of the statements in the first column. Decide if you agree or disagree with the statements. Record your opinion by marking an X in Agree or Disagree for each statement. Explain your choices in the fourth column. There are no right or wrong answers.

Statement	Agree	Disagree	Explain Your Answer
The American Dream is alive and well, and it is worth pursuing.			
There is no such thing as true love.			
It is always acceptable to go after what you want, even if you might hurt others in the process.			
Honesty is the best policy.			

Vocabulary Overview

Ten key words from this section are provided below with definitions and sentences about how the words are used in the book. Choose one of the vocabulary activity sheets (pages 15 or 16) for students to complete as they read this section. Monitor the students as they work to ensure the definitions they have found are accurate and relate to the text. Finally, discuss these important vocabulary words with the students. If you think these words or other words in the section warrant more time devoted to them, there are suggestions in the introduction for other vocabulary activities (page 5).

Word	Definition	Sentence about Text
supercilious (ch. 1)	disdainful; acting as if one thinks one is superior	Tom is a handsome man with a condescending, **supercilious** manner.
fractiousness (ch. 1)	being unruly; having no discipline	Many men at Yale avoided Tom because of his off-putting aura of **fractiousness**.
incredulously (ch. 1)	showing a lack of belief; skeptically	When Miss Baker says she can't drink because she is in training, Tom looks at her **incredulously**.
complacency (ch. 1)	feeling of uncritical satisfaction with one's self	Feelings of **complacency** can keep a person from improving himself.
contemptuous (ch. 1)	scornful; showing disdain	Nick is strangely attracted to Miss Baker's languid manner and **contemptuous** expression.
peremptorily (ch. 1)	leaving no opportunity for refusal	Confident Daisy stops Nick from leaving by calling out to him **peremptorily**.
discreetly (ch. 2)	showing self restraint; guarding one's privacy	To be **discreet**, Mrs. Wilson rides to the city in a different train car from Tom and Nick.
strident (ch. 2)	sounding harsh or unpleasant	The drunken partygoers repeatedly have **strident** arguments about nothing important.
simultaneously (ch. 2)	existing or occurring at the same time	Nick is **simultaneously** entertained and repelled by the wild party.
inexhaustible (ch. 2)	incapable of being used up	New York City seems to Nick to offer an **inexhaustible** variety of life and experiences.

© Shell Education

Name _____

Date _____

Understanding Vocabulary Words

Directions: The following words appear in this section of the book. Use context clues and reference materials to determine an accurate definition for each word.

Word	Definition
supercilious (ch. 1)	
fractiousness (ch. 1)	
incredulously (ch. 1)	
complacency (ch. 1)	
contemptuous (ch. 1)	
peremptorily (ch. 1)	
discreetly (ch. 2)	
strident (ch. 2)	
simultaneously (ch. 2)	
inexhaustible (ch. 2)	

Name _____

Date _____

During-Reading Vocabulary Activity

Directions: As you read these chapters, record at least eight important words on the lines below. Try to find interesting, difficult, intriguing, special, or funny words. Your words can be long or short. They can be hard or easy to spell. After each word, use context clues in the text and reference materials to define the word.

- _____
- _____
- _____
- _____
- _____
- _____
- _____
- _____
- _____
- _____

Directions: Respond to these questions about the words in this section.

1. What signs of **complacency** do you see in Daisy and/or Miss Baker?

   _____

   _____

2. Tom is not very **discreet** about his relationship with Myrtle. What does this say about Tom?

   _____

   _____

© Shell Education

Analyzing the Literature

Provided below are discussion questions you can use in small groups, with the whole class, or for written assignments. Each question is given at two levels so you can choose the right question for each group of students. Activity sheets with these questions are provided (pages 18–19) if you want students to write their responses. For each question, a few key discussion points are provided for your reference.

Story Element	■ Level 1	▲ Level 2	Key Discussion Points
Character	Nick gives directions to West Egg village to a newcomer and then realizes he is no longer lonely. Why do you think this is?	Nick identifies himself as a guide and a pathfinder. Why do you think Nick is pleased to see himself that way?	Discuss Nick's increasing curiosity and confidence here at the start of his stay in West Egg. He appears happy with his decision to move East. He comments that life seems to be starting anew for him, that a new chapter is opening. We get the sense that Nick is comfortable, at ease, and open to what life brings.
Setting	How does Fitzgerald describe West Egg and East Egg?	Explain how the author compares West Egg and East Egg. Why does Nick say there is a "sinister contrast" between them?	Fitzgerald describes West Egg as a less fashionable community, consisting of a number of garish homes built by the newly rich. East Egg is more refined and coveted, where established families have lived for generations. The areas represent the tension between "new money" and "old money."
Character	What do you know about the character of Gatsby at this point in the story?	Fitzgerald introduces Gatsby early in the story, but offers little information about him. Why does he choose to reveal Gatsby little by little?	Gatsby is mentioned as the resident of an enormous mansion, and Daisy seems to perk up when she hears his name. But neither Nick nor the reader know much about him except that he is wealthy and well known. The brief mentions make Gatsby seem mysterious and make the reader curious about him.
Plot	Why does the author give Tom a mistress? In what ways do you predict that this relationship might drive the novel's plot?	Does the description of Tom's extramarital relationship change the way you feel about Daisy? Do you think Daisy will take action in response to the affair?	Some may think that Tom and Daisy will separate. Others may believe Nick will get drawn into the unsavory group of Myrtle and her friends. Learning the extent of Tom's betrayal may make the reader more sympathetic to Daisy. Perhaps she is not spoiled and self absorbed, but rather sad and disillusioned.

Name _____

Date _____

Analyzing the Literature

Directions: Think about the section you have just read. Read each question and state your response with textual evidence.

1. Nick gives directions to West Egg village to a newcomer and then realizes he is no longer lonely. Why do you think this is?

   _____

   _____

   _____

   _____

2. How does Fitzgerald describe West Egg and East Egg?

   _____

   _____

   _____

   _____

3. What do you know about the character of Gatsby at this point in the story?

   _____

   _____

   _____

   _____

4. Why does the author give Tom a mistress? In what ways do you predict that this relationship might drive the novel's plot?

   _____

   _____

   _____

Name _____

Date _____

▲ Analyzing the Literature

Directions: Think about the section you have just read. Read each question and state your response with textual evidence.

1. Nick identifies himself as a guide and a pathfinder. Why do you think Nick is pleased to see himself that way?

    _____

    _____

    _____

    _____

2. Explain how the author compares West Egg and East Egg. Why does Nick say there is a "sinister contrast" between them?

    _____

    _____

    _____

    _____

3. Fitzgerald introduces Gatsby early in the story, but offers little information about him. Why does he choose to reveal Gatsby little by little?

    _____

    _____

    _____

4. Does the description of Tom's extramarital relationship change the way you feel about Daisy? Do you think Daisy will take action in response to the affair?

    _____

    _____

    _____

Name _____

Date _____

Reader Response

Directions: Choose one of the following prompts about this section to answer. Be sure you include a topic sentence in your response, use textual evidence to support your opinion, and provide a strong conclusion that summarizes your opinion.

Writing Prompts

- **Informative/Explanatory Piece**—*The Great Gatsby* depicts the culture of the 1920s in all its excess and opulence. Write about comparable examples of luxury you see in American culture today.
- **Narrative Piece**—At the end of chapter 2, Nick sees Gatsby standing on his lawn gazing across the water and holding out his arms toward a green light. Write an interior monologue for Gatsby in this moment.

_____

_____

_____

_____

_____

_____

_____

_____

_____

_____

_____

_____

_____

_____

Name _____

Date _____

Close Reading the Literature

Directions: Closely reread the section at the beginning of chapter 2 that begins, "About half way between West Egg and New York . . . ." Stop with, ". . . a damp gleam of hope sprang into his light blue eyes." Read each question below and then revisit the text to find evidence that supports your answer.

1. Based on the text, what is the "valley of ashes"? Describe it.

   _____

   _____

   _____

2. What mood does the author establish in this passage? Explain using specific language from the book.

   _____

   _____

   _____

3. Does Nick want to meet Tom's mistress? What clues in the text tell you this?

   _____

   _____

   _____

4. Why does Fitzgerald include the description of the eyes of Doctor T. J. Eckleburg? What does this advertisement represent?

   _____

   _____

   _____

   _____

Name _____

Date _____

Making Connections–What Does Great Really Mean

Directions: Fitzgerald titled the novel *The Great Gatsby*. Why do you think he chose this title? What do you think might be "great" about the main character? Think about and discuss the idea of greatness with your friends and family. Create a visually compelling graphic, such as a mind map, showing the qualities and specific behaviors of greatness. You might include mention of historical figures you consider "great" and examples of their actions.

© Shell Education

Name _____

Date _____

Creating with the Story Elements

Directions: Thinking about the story elements of character, setting, and plot in a novel is very important to understanding what is happening and why. Complete **one** of the following activities based on what you've read so far. Be creative and have fun!

Characters

Daisy talks with Nick about her daughter. In explaining her reaction to having a girl she says, "'All right' I said, 'I'm glad it's a girl. And I hope she'll be a fool—that's the best thing a girl can be in this world, a beautiful little fool.'" Write a letter or poem from Daisy to her daughter, giving advice or describing hopes for her future.

Setting

Choose a key scene from the novel to illustrate. Use creative software (e.g., *Photoshop* or *Microsoft Paint*), colored pencils, pastels, oils, or acrylic paint. Be sure to show through your illustration the qualities of mood and time Fitzgerald attempted to convey through his careful descriptions.

Plot

With a partner or small group, brainstorm five to eight predictions for the novel. Use a graphic organizer. Main categories might be "Relationship between Nick and Gatsby," "Relationship between Daisy and Tom," "How will Gatsby fit into the story?" etc. Consider how these story elements might shift and grow. Create a poster (digital or paper) showing your ideas and the reasoning behind them. Share it with the class.

Vocabulary Overview

Ten key words from this section are provided below with definitions and sentences about how the words are used in the book. Choose one of the vocabulary activity sheets (pages 25 or 26) for students to complete as they read this section. Monitor the students as they work to ensure the definitions they have found are accurate and relate to the text. Finally, discuss these important vocabulary words with the students. If you think these words or other words in the section warrant more time devoted to them, there are suggestions in the introduction for other vocabulary activities (page 5).

Word	Definition	Sentence about Text
gaudy (ch. 3)	bright and showy; not showing good taste	The guests at Gatsby's party fill the house with their colorful, **gaudy** dresses.
permeate (ch. 3)	to spread or flow throughout	At the free-wheeling party, rounds of cocktails quickly **permeate** the busy garden.
erroneous (ch. 3)	false or inaccurate	Rumors spread throughout the party, many of them **erroneous**.
vacuous (ch. 3)	showing a lack of intelligence or substance	As the night grows late, the laughter of the party goers gets louder and more **vacuous**.
corpulent (ch. 3)	fat	Nick expects Gatsby to be a **corpulent**, middle-aged man.
elicited (ch. 4)	drew forth	Nick is surprised to learn that Gatsby **elicited** a war decoration from the country of Montenegro.
incredulity (ch. 4)	being unable to believe something	Gatsby's eventful life story tests Nick's sense of **incredulity**.
denizen (ch. 4)	an inhabitant or citizen of a particular place	Meyer Wolfsheim is a true New Yorker, a **denizen** of Broadway.
unfathomable (ch. 4)	not able to be understood	At the beginning of her marriage, Daisy's love for Tom seems **unfathomably** deep.
disembodied (ch. 4)	free from bodily existence	Nick is happy to have the flesh-and-blood Jordan, rather than just a **disembodied** dream girl.

Name _____

Date _____

Understanding Vocabulary Words

Directions: The following words appear in this section of the book. Use context clues and reference materials to determine an accurate definition for each word.

Word	Definition
gaudy (ch. 3)	
permeate (ch. 3)	
erroneous (ch. 3)	
vacuous (ch. 3)	
corpulent (ch. 3)	
elicited (ch. 4)	
incredulity (ch. 4)	
denizen (ch. 4)	
unfathomable (ch. 4)	
disembodied (ch. 4)	

Name _____

Date _____

During-Reading Vocabulary Activity

Directions: As you read these chapters, record at least eight important words on the lines below. Try to find interesting, difficult, intriguing, special, or funny words. Your words can be long or short. They can be hard or easy to spell. After each word, use context clues in the text and reference materials to define the word.

- _____

- _____

- _____

- _____

- _____

- _____

- _____

- _____

Directions: Respond to these questions about the words in this section.

1. Why do the participants at Gatsby's parties **haughtily** gossip about his past, even suggesting he is a murderer and a German spy?

   _____

   _____

2. What **unfathomable** secret does Jordan learn from Gatsby the evening he steals her away for a private conversation?

   _____

   _____

Analyzing the Literature

Provided below are discussion questions you can use in small groups, with the whole class, or for written assignments. Each question is given at two levels so you can choose the right question for each group of students. Activity sheets with these questions are provided (pages 28–29) if you want students to write their responses. For each question, a few key discussion points are provided for your reference.

Story Element	■ Level 1	▲ Level 2	Key Discussion Points
Character	What is Nick's first impression of Gatsby?	Nick mentions that Gatsby speaks formally and picks his words carefully. What might this trait reveal about Gatsby's background?	Nick is surprised to find that the pleasant man with whom he has been speaking is Gatsby. He then notices Gatsby's rugged youth and awkward and forced formality. Gatsby's careful language might indicate that he was not raised in privilege, but rather he is new to high society. Later Nick sees something lonely and isolated in Gatsby as he stands alone at the party.
Setting	How does Nick describe Gatsby's rowdy summer parties?	In chapter 3, Nick gives a lengthy description of one of Gatsby's parties. What can you tell about how he views the people at the party?	Nick uses descriptive language to depict the lavishly long and luxurious party. There is lots of music and drinking and wild behavior. The partiers include streams of entitled people, many unknown to Gatsby, drinking to excess and behaving quite badly. Nick seems perplexed by much about the wild scene but still stays late to see it all.
Character	What has the reader learned about Nick so far in the story?	Nick shares his personality and perspective with the reader. Why is he an appropriate narrator for this story?	Readers know that Nick is from the Midwest, attended Yale, and fought in World War I. He recently moved east to learn the bond business. Nick is a keen observer; he seems to enjoy watching events unfold around him. He is fascinated by his cousin Daisy and his neighbor Gatsby. While he appears somewhat aggravated to be drawn into Gatsby's and Tom's activities, he does not avoid them, either.
Plot	Why does Gatsby enlist the support of Jordan and Nick in order to see Daisy?	Gatsby conceives of an elaborate plan to see Daisy. Why does he go to such great lengths to see her?	Gatsby has loved Daisy for years, despite her marriage to Tom. He purchases the mansion in West Egg to be near her. He throws the parties to impress her. Now, he wants to create a casual situation where Daisy comes into contact with him through people she trusts. Gatsby moves slowly and carefully because his whole life is focused on this possible reunion.

Name _____

Date _____

Analyzing the Literature

Directions: Think about the section you have just read. Read each question and state your response with textual evidence.

1. What is Nick's first impression of Gatsby?

_____

_____

_____

_____

2. How does Nick describe Gatsby's rowdy summer parties?

_____

_____

_____

_____

3. What has the reader learned about Nick so far in the story?

_____

_____

_____

_____

4. Why does Gatsby enlist the support of Jordan and Nick in order to see Daisy?

_____

_____

_____

_____

    © Shell Education

Name _____

Date _____

▲ Analyzing the Literature

Directions: Think about the section you have just read. Read each question and state your response with textual evidence.

1. Nick mentions that Gatsby speaks formally, and picks his words carefully. What might this trait reveal about Gatsby's background?

   _____

   _____

   _____

   _____

2. In chapter 3, Nick gives a lengthy description of one of Gatsby's parties. What can you tell about how he views the people at the party?

   _____

   _____

   _____

   _____

3. Nick shares his personality and perspective with the reader. Why is he an appropriate narrator for this story?

   _____

   _____

   _____

4. Gatsby conceives of an elaborate plan to see Daisy. Why does he go to such great lengths to see her?

   _____

   _____

   _____

Name _____

Date _____

Reader Response

Directions: Choose one of the following prompts about this section to answer. Be sure you include a topic sentence in your response, use textual evidence to support your opinion, and provide a strong conclusion that summarizes your opinion.

Writing Prompts

- **Argument Piece**—Do you like Nick as a person? Why or why not?
- **Narrative Piece**—Take on the character of Gatsby. Write a diary entry showing your hopes about Daisy and your plans to get her to your home in West Egg. Be sure to write in Gatsby's voice.

_____

_____

_____

_____

_____

_____

_____

_____

_____

_____

_____

_____

_____

_____

_____

Name _____

Date _____

Close Reading the Literature

Directions: Closely reread the section in chapter 4 that begins, "Well, I'm going to tell you something about my life." Stop with, "You'll hear about it this afternoon." Read each question below and then revisit the text to find evidence that supports your answer.

1. Why does Nick think Gatsby is lying when he says he was educated at Oxford? Use specifics from the text.

   _____

   _____

   _____

2. At first, Nick has a hard time keeping himself from laughing at Gatsby's tale. What is he picturing as Gatsby goes on?

   _____

   _____

   _____

3. What two pieces of evidence convince Nick that Gatsby's life story is the truth after all?

   _____

   _____

   _____

4. Based on the book, why does Gatsby care whether Nick knows about his past?

   _____

   _____

   _____

Name _____

Date _____

Making Connections—Public Perceptions

Directions: Several people who attend Gatsby's parties gossip openly about him. We see that no one really knows much about Gatsby at all. One guest claims he is a murderer. Another says he is a German spy. Jordan says she doesn't believe Gatsby attended Oxford.

1. Why do you think so many of Gatsby's guests spread rumors about him?

_____

_____

_____

_____

2. Where do you see gossip and rumors in your own community? Give examples.

_____

_____

_____

_____

3. What are some negative side effects of gossip and other kinds of negative talk?

_____

_____

_____

4. What are some ways a group of friends, a class, or a larger community can reduce the spread of gossip?

_____

_____

_____

    © Shell Education

Name _____

Date _____

Creating with the Story Elements

Directions: Thinking about the story elements of character, setting, and plot in a novel is very important to understanding what is happening and why. Complete **one** of the following activities based on what you've read so far. Be creative and have fun!

Characters

Create and perform or record your version of the private dialogue between Jordan and Gatsby during his party. Be sure to include the story Gatsby tells Jordan and the favor he asks of her. Pay attention to portraying their characters through your choice of words.

Setting

Create a soundtrack for the scene where Gatsby and Nick drive to New York City together. Be sure to consider the fancy automobile, the changing scenery, the conversation, and the two characters as you make your music selections.

Language

Write a found poem. Using favorite language you find in chapters 3 and 4, draft a poem reflecting the novel in some way. Your poem may connect to a character, a theme, a place, or an event in the story.

Vocabulary Overview

Ten key words from this section are provided below with definitions and sentences about how the words are used in the book. Choose one of the vocabulary activity sheets (pages 35 or 36) for students to complete as they read this section. Monitor students as they work to ensure the definitions they have found are accurate and relate to the text. Finally, discuss these important vocabulary words with students. If you think these words or other words in the section warrant more time devoted to them, there are suggestions in the introduction for other vocabulary activities (page 5).

Word	Definition	Sentence about Text
suppressed (ch. 5)	subdued	Gatsby waits with barely **suppressed** eagerness to see if Nick will ask Daisy to tea.
innumerable (ch. 5)	too many to be numbered or counted	Before tea with Daisy, Gatsby fills Nick's house with **innumerable** flower arrangements.
defunct (ch. 5)	having finished the course of life; dead	Gatsby accidentally knocks over an old, **defunct** mantelpiece clock.
obstinate (ch. 5)	sticking to an opinion or course of action despite reason or persuasion; stubborn	Nick tells a story about Gatsby's elaborate house and points out that Americans can be **obstinate** about issues of class.
nebulous (ch. 5)	unclear, hazy	Mr. Klipspringer dons well-worn trousers that have faded to a **nebulous** hue.
laudable (ch. 6)	praiseworthy; notable	The young reporter, showing **laudable** initiative, arrives at Gatsby's doorstep.
insidious (ch. 6)	treacherous	Gatsby warns Dan Cody that his yacht is anchored on an **insidious** spot.
ineffable (ch. 6)	impossible to describe with words	Young Gatsby dreams of a life of **ineffable** luxury and excitement.
obtrusive (ch. 6)	noticeable; prominent	Daisy is appalled by the gaudy, overly **obtrusive** behavior of the West Egg partygoers.
elusive (ch. 6)	hard to capture or define	Nick struggles to grasp an **elusive** memory, but it slips away.

© *Shell Education*

Name _____

Date _____

Understanding Vocabulary Words

Directions: The following words appear in this section of the book. Use context clues and reference materials to determine an accurate definition for each word.

Word	Definition
suppressed (ch. 5)	
innumerable (ch. 5)	
defunct (ch. 5)	
obstinate (ch. 5)	
nebulous (ch. 5)	
laudable (ch. 6)	
insidious (ch. 6)	
ineffable (ch. 6)	
obtrusive (ch. 6)	
elusive (ch. 6)	

Name _____

Date _____

During-Reading Vocabulary Activity

Directions: As you read these chapters, record at least eight important words on the lines below. Try to find interesting, difficult, intriguing, special, or funny words. Your words can be long or short. They can be hard or easy to spell. After each word, use context clues in the text and reference materials to define the word.

- _____

- _____

- _____

- _____

- _____

- _____

- _____

- _____

- _____

- _____

Directions: Now, organize your words. Rewrite each of the words on a sticky note. Work with a group to create a bar graph of your words. Stack any words that are the same on top of one another. Different words should appear in different columns. Finally, discuss with the group why certain words were chosen more often than other words.

                    © Shell Education

Analyzing the Literature

Provided below are discussion questions you can use in small groups, with the whole class, or for written assignments. Each question is given at two levels so you can choose the right question for each group of students. Activity sheets with these questions are provided (pages 38–39) if you want students to write their responses. For each question, a few key discussion points are provided for your reference.

Story Element	■ Level 1	▲ Level 2	Key Discussion Points
Plot	In chapter 5, Gatsby finally sees Daisy again. How might this event change the plotline of the story?	There is a turning point in the story in this section of the novel. What is it and how does it shift the plotline?	Gatsby and Daisy finally meet, after a lengthy build up. Their mutual interest is rekindled, and Nick notes that both are joyful and excited. The reader might wonder whether they will start an affair, and what will happen with Daisy and Tom. There may be questions about Nick's future and his growing friendship with Gatsby.
Setting	How does Daisy respond to Gatsby's personal tour of his home?	How does Gatsby's house tour with Daisy and Nick change the way Daisy views Gatsby? Why is this important?	Daisy is astonished and impressed by Gatsby's new wealth and taste. She sees that he is a rich man with an interest in the finer things. Her appreciation reaches a peak when she cries over his gaudy display of piles of European silk shirts. Gatsby feels great joy that his efforts to remake his persona seem to have been worth it.
Theme	Tom and his friend Mr. Sloane visit Gatsby's home but are disrespectful to their host. Why do they treat Gatsby poorly?	How does Fitzgerald raise issues of social class in these chapters?	Gatsby is introduced to wealth in his teen years when he works for Dan Cody. This sparks his drive to go from rags to riches. But money cannot fully eclipse the divide of social class. We see this when Tom and Mr. Sloane snub Gatsby, whom they consider beneath them, and when Tom and Daisy come to a party at Gatsby's and are appalled by much of what they see.
Character	Why does Nick warn Gatsby not to try to repeat the past with Daisy?	Nick finds "appalling sentimentality" in Gatsby's memories of Daisy. Why is he concerned about his friend's unrealistic attitude?	Nick sees Gatsby holding on to a vision of Daisy and their relationship that is more than five years old. Nick believes that Gatsby is attempting to recapture the past and he knows it to be impossible. He also knows that Daisy will fall short of Gatsby's unattainable memory of her.

Name _____

Date _____

Analyzing the Literature

Directions: Think about the section you have just read. Read each question and state your response with textual evidence.

1. In chapter 5, Gatsby finally sees Daisy again. How might this event change the plotline of the story?

   _____

   _____

   _____

   _____

2. How does Daisy respond to Gatsby's personal tour of his home?

   _____

   _____

   _____

3. Tom and his friend Mr. Sloane visit Gatsby's home but are disrespectful to their host. Why do they treat Gatsby poorly?

   _____

   _____

   _____

4. Why does Nick warn Gatsby not to try to repeat the past with Daisy?

   _____

   _____

   _____

Name _____

Date _____

▲ Analyzing the Literature

Directions: Think about the section you have just read. Read each question and state your response with textual evidence.

1. There is a turning point in the story in this section of the novel. What is it and how does it shift the plotline?

   _____

   _____

   _____

   _____

2. How does Gatsby's house tour with Daisy and Nick change the way Daisy views Gatsby? Why is this important?

   _____

   _____

   _____

   _____

3. How does Fitzgerald raise issues of social class in these chapters?

   _____

   _____

   _____

   _____

4. Nick finds "appalling sentimentality" in Gatsby's memories of Daisy. Why is he concerned about his friend's unrealistic attitude?

   _____

   _____

   _____

Name _____

Date _____

Reader Response

Directions: Choose one of the following prompts about this section to answer. Be sure you include a topic sentence in your response, use textual evidence to support your opinion, and provide a strong conclusion that summarizes your opinion.

Writing Prompts

- **Argument Piece**—According to Nick, "You can't repeat the past." But Gatsby retorts, "Why of course you can!" Defend one of these positions with examples from your own life.
- **Informative/Explanatory Piece**—Dan Cody has a life-altering impact on Gatsby. Write a blog post or column for the school newspaper about how mentors can make a difference.

_____

_____

_____

_____

_____

_____

_____

_____

_____

_____

_____

_____

Name _____

Date _____

Close Reading the Literature

Directions: Closely reread the section where Daisy, Gatsby, and Nick are in the middle of Gatsby's house tour beginning with, "After the house . . . ." Stop reading at the close of the chapter. Read each question below and then revisit the text to find evidence that supports your answer.

1. Gatsby shares the significance of the green light. What is it and what does Daisy do in response?

   _____

   _____

   _____

2. Nick says that his presence might have made Gatsby and Daisy feel more alone with their privacy. How can this be?

   _____

   _____

   _____

3. Based on the conversation included in the book, what kind of phone call does Gatsby receive during this scene? Why does he end the call so quickly?

   _____

   _____

   _____

4. What does Nick mean when he says, "No amount of fire or freshness can challenge what a man can store up in his ghostly heart"?

   _____

   _____

   _____

Name _____

Date _____

Making Connections– The Pros and Cons of Wealth

Directions: Wealth is a central theme in this novel, which features main players obsessed with money and power in individual ways. Talk with your friends and family about their ideas of wealth. Research stories on wealth in our country or in your community. Compose your own personal position on wealth and/or the pursuit of wealth. Then, answer the prompts below.

1. Ask three people—friends, teachers, or family members—what they think about how wealth is viewed in our society. Describe their responses.

   _____

   _____

   _____

   _____

2. Where do you see positive outcomes of wealth and its power? Where do you see negative outcomes of wealth?

   _____

   _____

   _____

   _____

3. What are your personal feelings about the use of money and how it connects and does not connect to happiness?

   _____

   _____

   _____

   _____

© Shell Education

Name _____

Date _____

Creating with the Story Elements

Directions: Thinking about the story elements of character, setting, and plot in a novel is very important to understanding what is happening and why. Complete **one** of the following activities based on what you've read so far. Be creative and have fun!

Characters

Assume the character of Daisy. Write a letter from Daisy to Jordan in which she reflects upon her afternoon at Nick's house with Gatsby and the tour of his home. Be sure to include any of her expectations, surprises, and thoughts about the days ahead.

Setting

Reread the party scene or the home tour Gatsby gives to Daisy and Nick. Create an advertising campaign for the fashion designer responsible for the most striking clothing, the interior designer who outfitted Gatsby's home, or the landscape architect who designed the outdoor spaces and gardens. Draft the voiceover monologue for the product in a piece of writing or a podcast. Create an accompanying 2D visual using your choice of medium (ink, paint, digital).

Plot

Write, perform, and, if possible, videotape a dialogue between Dan Cody and the 17-year-old Gatsby, showing the nature of their mentor/mentee relationship. How did Gatsby impress Cody? How did Cody captivate Gatsby? Show the kind of relationship you think they had. Detail any plans they may have had before Cody's untimely death.

Vocabulary Overview

Ten key words from this section are provided below with definitions and sentences about how the words are used in the book. Choose one of the vocabulary activity sheets (pages 45 or 46) for students to complete as they read this section. Monitor the students as they work to ensure the definitions they have found are accurate and relate to the text. Finally, discuss these important vocabulary words with the students. If you think these words or other words in the section warrant more time devoted to them, there are suggestions in the introduction for other vocabulary activities (page 5).

Word	Definition	Sentence about Text
affront (ch. 7)	an offensive action or word	It is so hot outside that Nick thinks every extra action is an **affront** to his well-being.
relinquished (ch. 7)	let go of; released	The nurse **relinquishes** Daisy's daughter and the child runs to see her mother.
boisterously (ch. 7)	noisily; in a carefree way	Tom **boisterously** brushes aside Gatsby's concerns.
inviolate (ch. 7)	pure; safe from violation or injury	Tom is shocked to learn that his comfortable life is not as **inviolate** as he assumed.
precipitately (ch. 7)	suddenly	The shocking events of the day make Tom feel as if his life is slipping **precipitately** from his control.
portentous (ch. 7)	overly solemn	The **portentous** strains of the "Wedding March" can be heard from the ballroom below.
libertine (ch. 7)	a person who behaves without moral principles	Nick wants to laugh when the **libertine** Tom falsely presents himself as a moral authority.
vicariously (ch. 7)	experienced by watching, not by doing it oneself	Tom and Daisy think others should be pleased to **vicariously** experience their emotions.
rancor (ch. 7)	a bitter, angry feeling of hatred	After her brief burst of anger, the **rancor** disappears from Daisy's voice.
magnanimous (ch. 7)	being generous or forgiving	Once he knows he has won, Tom is **magnanimous** towards Gatsby.

© Shell Education

Name _____

Date _____

Understanding Vocabulary Words

Directions: The following words appear in this section of the book. Use context clues and reference materials to determine an accurate definition for each word.

Word	Definition
affront (ch. 7)	
relinquished (ch. 7)	
boisterously (ch. 7)	
inviolate (ch. 7)	
precipitately (ch. 7)	
portentous (ch. 7)	
libertine (ch. 7)	
vicariously (ch. 7)	
rancor (ch. 7)	
magnanimous (ch. 7)	

Name _____

Date _____

During-Reading Vocabulary Activity

Directions: As you read these chapters, record at least eight important words on the lines below. Try to find interesting, difficult, intriguing, special, or funny words. Your words can be long or short. They can be hard or easy to spell. After each word, use context clues in the text and reference materials to define the word.

- _____

- _____

- _____

- _____

- _____

- _____

- _____

- _____

Directions: Respond to these questions about the words in this section.

1. The **portentous** notes of Mendelssohn's "Wedding March" play as Gatsby and Tom argue about Daisy. What ironic symbolism does this have?

   _____

   _____

2. Nick indicates that the Buchanans consider it a privilege for others to partake **vicariously** of their emotions. What does that tell you about how he views the couple?

   _____

   _____

    © Shell Education

Analyzing the Literature

Provided below are discussion questions you can use in small groups, with the whole class, or for written assignments. Each question is given at two levels so you can choose the right question for each group of students. Activity sheets with these questions are provided (pages 48–49) if you want students to write their responses. For each question, a few key discussion points are provided for your reference.

Story Element	■ Level 1	▲ Level 2	Key Discussion Points
Character	How does Tom react to finding out about Daisy and Gatsby's relationship?	Are Daisy and Gatsby careful to conceal their affair from Tom? What motivation does each have to allow the relationship to surface?	Daisy and Gatsby show affection openly both in the Buchanan home and at the Plaza Hotel. All present see the nature of their romantic relationship. Gatsby is motivated by love. Daisy feels love but may also want to make her husband jealous. At first, Tom is astounded. Then he becomes angry and challenging. Tom reminds Daisy of better times and promises to be more devoted. He manipulates her skillfully.
Setting	Why is a fancy hotel a suitable setting for the confrontation between Tom, Daisy, and Gatsby?	How is it appropriate that the group ends up at the ritzy Plaza Hotel for the confrontation scene?	The famous Plaza Hotel is an appropriate setting for this showy, wealthy group of people. It fits their character to spend money on an expensive room simply because they didn't know what else to do with themselves. Additionally, the author may have wanted a neutral space away from West Egg and East Egg for the showdown between Gatsby and Tom.
Character	How do Nick's attitudes towards Daisy, Tom, Gatsby, and even Jordan develop in this chapter?	What do the observations Nick makes throughout this chapter tell you about how he has come to view his friends?	Students should note that Nick includes the details and nuances of the characters' behavior, their expressions, emotions and interactions. He grows increasingly disgusted with the flagrant behavior, which culminates in the death of Myrtle, writing that he is done with them. Nick rejects Jordan's invitation to continue the evening and places his head in his hands.
Plot	At the end of chapter 7, does there seem to be any hope for a happy ending to this story?	Myrtle's sudden death will affect the plotline of the story. What do you think will happen next?	A happy ending seems unlikely, as Daisy appears to have turned her back on Gatsby, Nick is newly disillusioned, and Myrtle's tragic death hangs over the characters. Students should discuss the likely behavior and the fates of all the main characters.

Name _____

Date _____

Analyzing the Literature

Directions: Think about the section you have just read. Read each question and state your response with textual evidence.

1. How does Tom react to finding out about Daisy and Gatsby's relationship?

_____

_____

_____

_____

2. Why is a fancy hotel a suitable setting for the confrontation between Tom, Daisy, and Gatsby?

_____

_____

_____

_____

3. How do Nick's attitudes towards Daisy, Tom, Gatsby, and even Jordan develop in this chapter?

_____

_____

_____

_____

4. At the end of chapter 7, does there seem to be any hope for a happy ending to this story?

_____

_____

_____

Name _____

Date _____

▲ Analyzing the Literature

Directions: Think about the section you have just read. Read each question and state your response with textual evidence.

1. Are Daisy and Gatsby careful to conceal their affair from Tom? What motivation does each have to allow the relationship to surface?

_____

_____

_____

_____

2. How is it appropriate that the group ends up at the ritzy Plaza Hotel for the confrontation scene?

_____

_____

_____

_____

3. What do the observations Nick makes throughout this chapter tell you about how he has come to view his friends?

_____

_____

_____

4. Myrtle's sudden death will affect the plotline of the story. What do you think will happen next?

_____

_____

_____

Name _____

Date _____

Reader Response

Directions: Choose one of the following prompts about this section to answer. Be sure you include a topic sentence in your response, use textual evidence to support your opinion, and provide a strong conclusion that summarizes your opinion.

Writing Prompts

- **Narrative Piece**—Gatsby uses the phrase "old sport" throughout the novel. What are common phrases you use with your friends? Rewrite some dialogue from the novel using popular current slang.
- **Informative/Explanatory Piece**—Myrtle is violently killed. Where else do you see Fitzgerald using violence? What point does the author want to make about violence?

_____

_____

_____

_____

_____

_____

_____

_____

_____

_____

_____

_____

_____

    © Shell Education

Name _____

Date _____

Close Reading the Literature

Directions: Closely reread the section in chapter 7 that begins with Tom commanding, "I want to know what Mr. Gatsby has to tell me." Stop with, "'You can suit yourself about that, old sport' said Gatsby steadily." Read each question below and then revisit the text to find evidence that supports your answer.

1. Why does Gatsby tell Tom that Daisy, his wife, never really loved him? What impact does this statement have?

   _____

   _____

   _____

2. Use examples from the text to explain how Daisy reacts to the struggle between Gatsby and Tom.

   _____

   _____

   _____

3. What term does Tom use to describe, and play down the importance of, his philandering?

   _____

   _____

   _____

4. Specifically, what strategies does Tom use to lessen Daisy's respect for Gatsby?

   _____

   _____

   _____

Name _____

Date _____

Making Connections—Gender Roles and Power

Directions: Fitzgerald raises some interesting questions about gender roles, power, and double standards in *The Great Gatsby*. Compare Daisy and Jordan with the women you know today. How have things changed for women? Is there complete equality for men and women today? On the chart below, compare some differences in roles for women then vs. now.

Women in the 1920s	Women Today

© Shell Education

Name _____

Date _____

Creating with the Story Elements

Directions: Thinking about the story elements of character, setting, and plot in a novel is very important to understanding what is happening and why. Complete **one** of the following activities based on what you've read so far. Be creative and have fun!

Characters

Write an interior monologue for Daisy during the disturbing scene in the hotel room at the Plaza Hotel, where both Gatsby and Tom make declarations about Daisy's true feelings. Stay in character. Present Daisy's innermost thoughts during these moments.

Setting

Fitzgerald chooses to hold the showdown between Gatsby and Tom at the Plaza Hotel. What other settings might have worked for such a scene? A famous horse race? An exclusive cruise in a hired yacht? Choose another setting and situation. Rewrite the scene where Tom and Gatsby fight over Daisy's love. Share your scene on a fan fiction site.

Plot

Using events, characters, themes, and descriptions of the story so far, create a poster that represents the spirit of the novel. Include the elements of the story that have been the most striking or intriguing for you so far. On the back of your poster, write a brief prediction about how the story might end.

Vocabulary Overview

Ten key words from this section are provided below with definitions and sentences about how the words are used in the book. Choose one of the vocabulary activity sheets (pages 55 or 56) for students to complete as they read this section. Monitor the students as they work to ensure the definitions they have found are accurate and relate to the text. Finally, discuss these important vocabulary words with the students. If you think these words or other words in the section warrant more time devoted to them, there are suggestions in the introduction for other vocabulary activities (page 5).

Word	Definition	Sentence about Text
incessantly (ch. 8)	constantly; nonstop	Nick cannot sleep because a fog-horn groans **incessantly** on the sound.
redolent (ch. 8)	suggestive of something	To a young Gatsby, Daisy's very home seems **redolent** of a rich, full life.
unscrupulously (ch. 8)	unprincipled; without being honest or fair	Gatsby **unscrupulously** presents himself to Daisy as a more established man.
interminable (ch. 8)	seemingly endless	A preoccupied Nick tries to make his way through a seemingly **interminable** pile of work.
garrulous (ch. 8)	overly talkative	Nick avoids the scene of the accident, fearing he will have to deal with **garrulous** bystanders.
surmise (ch. 9)	an idea that is based on little or no evidence	Gatsby's death only increases the number of **surmises** made about him.
superfluous (ch. 9)	more than what is enough or necessary; extra	Nick is wrong when he assumes that his letter to Mr. Wolfsheim is **superfluous**.
scrutinized (ch. 9)	examined very closely; inspected	The secretary **scrutinizes** Nick as he insists on speaking to Mr. Wolfsheim.
indignantly (ch. 9)	expressing strong displeasure	**Indignantly**, the secretary asks Nick to leave the office.
incoherent (ch. 9)	not logical or organized; disjointed	Nick describes Gatsby's house as an **incoherent** failure.

© Shell Education

Name _____

Date _____

Understanding Vocabulary Words

Directions: The following words appear in this section of the book. Use context clues and reference materials to determine an accurate definition for each word.

Word	Definition
incessantly (ch. 8)	
redolent (ch. 8)	
unscrupulously (ch. 8)	
interminable (ch. 8)	
garrulous (ch. 8)	
surmise (ch. 9)	
superfluous (ch. 9)	
scrutinized (ch. 9)	
indignantly (ch. 9)	
incoherent (ch. 9)	

Name _____

Date _____

During-Reading Vocabulary Activity

Directions: As you read these chapters, choose five important words from the story. Then, use those five words to complete this word flow chart. On each arrow, write a vocabulary word. In the boxes between the words, explain how the words connect. An example has been done for you using the words *incoherent* and *surmises*.

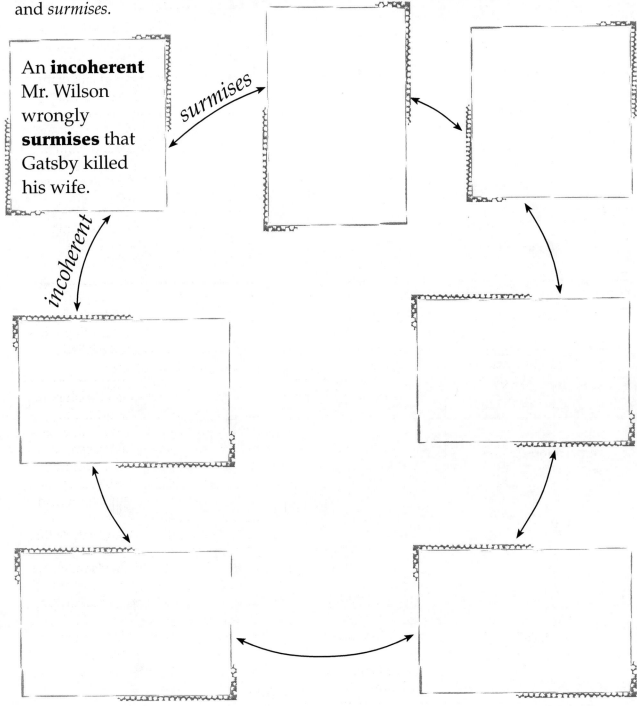

An **incoherent** Mr. Wilson wrongly **surmises** that Gatsby killed his wife.

surmises

incoherent

© Shell Education

Analyzing the Literature

Provided below are discussion questions you can use in small groups, with the whole class, or for written assignments. Each question is given at two levels so you can choose the right question for each group of students. Activity sheets with these questions are provided (pages 58–59) if you want students to write their responses. For each question, a few key discussion points are provided for your reference.

Story Element	■ Level 1	▲ Level 2	Key Discussion Points
Character	Why does Nick tell Gatsby that he is better than all the rest of their friends put together?	Although Nick admits to disapproving of Gatsby, he obviously also sees virtue in the man. What does Nick see in his friend that others might miss?	Nick sees in Gatsby a desire to be more pure and more generous than other players in the story. While Gatsby may be involved in illegal financial affairs, he does this out of love. The others in the story seem much more shallow, motivated by greed, lust, and vanity. They are guilty of being careless with others' feelings, while Gatsby cares too much and gives too much.
Theme	Despite his earlier plans, Nick returns to the "Middle West" after Gatsby's funeral. Why does he leave the East?	Fitzgerald contrasts the Midwest and the East. At the end of the story he sends Nick back home. What statement do you think he is making by doing this?	Nick speaks warmly about growing up in the Midwest. The fast pace and consumer culture of the East is presented, in contrast, as a corrupting influence. Nick hopes to escape the ugliness he has witnessed in Gatsby, Tom, Daisy, and others by leaving what he sees as the shallow, materialistic culture of the East.
Setting	Why does the author set Gatsby's death in his swimming pool?	Gatsby delays having the pool drained because he hasn't used it. Soon after, he is shot in the pool. How does this juxtaposition serve the themes of the novel?	Owning and maintaining a lavish pool, while never using it, highlights the excesses of the age and the shallowness of materialism. Things alone cannot bring love and happiness. Ironically, Gatsby dies in the pool he never found time to enjoy. There is also symbolism inherent in the end of summer coinciding with the end of Gatsby's life.
Plot	Why do so few people show up to Gatsby's funeral?	Nick tries to get out the word about Gatsby's funeral. But only a few people are willing to attend. Why do the crowds forsake Gatsby after his death?	Most people went to Gatsby's mansion for selfish purposes, to attend all the fancy parties and enjoy the seemingly endless hospitality in his grand home. They used their host for his money and connections. No one but Daisy and Nick were truly close to Gatsby. Many didn't even know who he was.

Name _____

Date _____

Analyzing the Literature

Directions: Think about the section you have just read. Read each question and state your response with textual evidence.

1. Why does Nick tell Gatsby that he is better than all the rest of their friends put together?

_____

_____

_____

_____

2. Despite his earlier plans, Nick returns to the "Middle West" after Gatsby's funeral. Why does he leave the East?

_____

_____

_____

_____

3. Why does the author set Gatsby's death in his swimming pool?

_____

_____

_____

_____

4. Why do so few people show up to Gatsby's funeral?

_____

_____

_____

© Shell Education

Name _____

Date _____

▲ Analyzing the Literature

Directions: Think about the section you have just read. Read each question and state your response with textual evidence.

1. Although Nick admits to disapproving of Gatsby, he obviously also sees virtue in the man. What does Nick see in his friend that others might miss?

   _____

   _____

   _____

   _____

2. Fitzgerald contrasts the Midwest and the East. At the end of the story he sends Nick back home. What statement do you think he is making by doing this?

   _____

   _____

   _____

3. Gatsby delays having the pool drained because he hasn't used it all summer. Soon after, he is shot in the pool. How does this juxtaposition serve the themes of the novel?

   _____

   _____

   _____

4. Nick tries to get out the word about Gatsby's funeral. But only a few people are willing to attend. Why do the crowds forsake Gatsby after his death?

   _____

   _____

   _____

Name _____

Date _____

Reader Response

Directions: Choose one of the following prompts about this section to answer. Be sure you include a topic sentence in your response, use textual evidence to support your opinion, and provide a strong conclusion that summarizes your opinion.

Writing Prompts

- **Argument Piece**—Life in New York was exhilarating during the Roaring Twenties. Write about why you would, or would not, like to have lived in this time and place.
- **Informative/Explanatory Piece**—Nick tells Gatsby that, "They're a rotten crowd," and that Gatsby is worth all of them put together. Using Nick's voice, write a eulogy with this sentiment for Gatsby.

_____

_____

_____

_____

_____

_____

_____

_____

_____

_____

_____

_____

Name _____

Date _____

Close Reading the Literature

Directions: Closely reread the passage in chapter 8 that begins, "When I passed the ashheaps . . . ." Stop with, ". . . nodding into the twilight." Read each question below and then revisit the text to find evidence that supports your answer.

1. At 3:00, Wilson's "incoherent muttering" changes into something else. What does he start talking about?

   _____

   _____

   _____

2. What seemingly innocuous item, mentioned in the text, made it clear to Wilson that his wife was having an affair? Why was it revealing?

   _____

   _____

   _____

3. Throughout the night, Wilson works himself up to a conclusion about the reason for the fatal car accident. Eventually, what does he proclaim?

   _____

   _____

   _____

4. Based on the text, in what surprising way does Wilson describe the advertisement for Doctor T. J. Eckleburg?

   _____

   _____

   _____

Name _____

Date _____

Making Connections–The Roaring 1920s

Directions: *The Great Gatsby* takes place during the 1920s. Even though it is a fictional piece of literature, many of the places and customs described in the book accurately reflect that time period. Here is a list of some of the phenomena of the age. Choose one topic to research. Write an essay discussing the historical significance of the item and how the topic connects to our culture today.

- The Jazz Age
- The Rise of Consumer Culture
- Women's Rights
- The Automobile
- Prohibition

_____

_____

_____

_____

_____

_____

_____

_____

_____

_____

_____

_____

_____

_____

© Shell Education

Name _____

Date _____

Creating with the Story Elements

Directions: Thinking about the story elements of character, setting, and plot in a novel is very important to understanding what is happening and why. Complete **one** of the following activities based on what you've read so far. Be creative and have fun!

Characters

Imagine you have the opportunity to interview Daisy well after Gatsby's death. Draft a list of questions you would like to ask her. Write responses to the questions using her voice. Write a profile article about Daisy, including this interview. Be sure you stay true to her character as you write her answers. Share your article on a fan fiction site, class blog or wiki.

Setting

After Gatsby's death, his house sits abandoned. The grass grows too long, graffiti appears, and the place takes on an air of neglect. Nick describes the place as "that huge incoherent failure of a house." Imagine that you are a real estate agent given the opportunity to sell Gatsby's home. Create a listing that describes the home, making mention of the location, the interior, and the exterior. Think about what you would write if you really wanted to make the home attractive to prospective buyers. Create a drawing of the house to attach to your listing.

Plot

The American Dream promises that the opportunity for prosperity, success, and happiness is available to all people in America, no matter where they start in life. However, Jay Gatsby's pursuit of the American Dream ends in tragedy. Write an alternative narrative for the life of Jay Gatz. In this lifetime, assume he never meets Daisy. How might his motivations, decisions, and achievements have differed? Would he have had a better chance at the American Dream?

Name _____

Date _____

Post-Reading Theme Thoughts

Directions: Read each of the statements in the first column. Choose a main character from *The Great Gatsby*. Think about that character's point of view. From that character's perspective, decide if the character would agree or disagree with the statement. Record the character's opinion by marking an X in Agree or Disagree for each statement. Explain your choices in the fourth column using text evidence.

Character I Chose: _____

Statement	Agree	Disagree	Explain Your Answer
The American Dream is alive and well, and it is worth pursuing.			
There is no such thing as true love.			
It is always acceptable to go after what you want, even if you might hurt others in the process.			
Honesty is the best policy.			

    © Shell Education

Name _____

Date _____

Culminating Activity:
Jay Gatsby, a Complex Character

Directions: With a partner or in a small group, discuss your understanding of Jay Gatsby as a person. Create a Venn diagram that displays both his positive and his negative actions and personality characteristics. Show that some aspects of his character can be seen as both positive and negative. Compare and discuss your findings with your classmates.

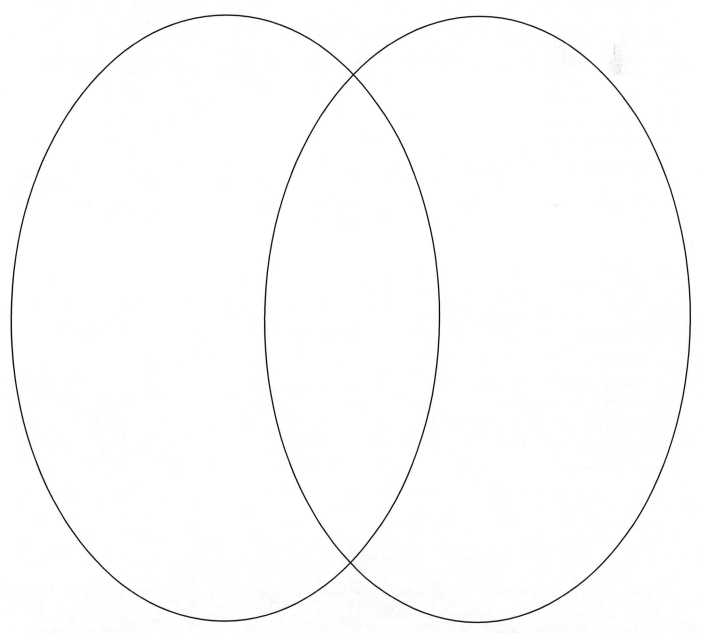

Name _____

Date _____

Culminating Activity:
Six-Word Memoir for Jay Gatsby

Directions: Using some of the ideas about Gatsby you noted in the last activity, write a couple six-word memoirs for him. (See some examples below.) Next to your six-word memoirs create a visual that artfully shows who Gatsby was and what his life was about.

Sample Six-Word Memoirs

I was terrified. Did it anyway.

Sketchy past has people drawing conclusions.

A runaway train with a destination.

_____

_____

_____

_____

_____

    © Shell Education

Name _____

Date _____

Comprehension Assessment

Directions: Circle the letter for the best response to each question.

1. What is the main idea of this statement from Nick, which opens the novel?

   "In my younger and more vulnerable years my father gave me some advice that I've been turning over in my mind ever since. 'Whenever you feel like criticizing any one,' he told me, 'just remember that all the people in this world haven't had the advantages that you've had.'"

   _____

   _____

2. Choose **two** details to support your answer to number 1.

   A. Nick disapproves of Gatsby's flamboyant lifestyle but cannot help but like him as a person.

   B. Gatsby changed his name from James Gatz to Jay Gatsby to hide from Dan Cody.

   C. Jordan describes Daisy's voice as being "full of money."

   D. Nick comes from a prominent, well-to-do family in the Midwest.

3. How does Nick's opinion of the Buchanans change from the beginning of the novel to the end?

   E. Nick first thinks they are boring but later finds them interesting.

   F. Nick first thinks they are fascinating but later finds them reprehensible.

   G. Nick first thinks they are vulgar but later finds them sophisticated.

   H. Nick first thinks they are silly but later finds them intelligent.

4. What observation from the book provides the best evidence for your answer to number 3?

   A. ". . . it occurred to me that there was no difference between men, in intelligence or race, so profound as the difference between the sick and the well."

   B. "She had told him she loved him, and Tom Buchanan saw.

   C. "They were careless people, Tom and Daisy—they smashed up things and creatures and then retreated back into their money . . . ."

   D. "It was touching to see them together—it made you laugh in a hushed, fascinated way."

Comprehension Assessment (cont.)

5. Why is Gatsby's pursuit of Daisy doomed to fail?

    E. Daisy is not interested in Gatsby.

    F. The past love between Daisy and Gatsby cannot be recaptured.

    G. Daisy is committed to faithfulness to her husband Tom.

    H. Daisy plans to run off with Nick.

6. On page 118, a restless Daisy exclaims, "What'll we do with ourselves this afternoon? . . . and the day after that, and the next thirty years?" What does this outburst reveal about Daisy's world view?

    _____

    _____

    _____

    _____

    _____

7. Which statement best expresses a central theme of the book?

    A. People often surprise you.

    B. Having many moneyed friends brings social status and self-satisfaction.

    C. No matter how hard we try, we cannot ever truly escape our past.

    D. True love is more important than anything that might get in its way.

8. What detail provides the best evidence for your answer to number 7?

    E. "So we beat on, boats against the current, borne back ceaselessly into the past."

    F. "You see I usually find myself among strangers because I drift here and there trying to forget the sad things that happened to me."

    G. "There are only the pursued, the pursuing, the busy and the tired."

    H. "All I kept thinking about, over and over, was 'You can't live forever; you can't live forever.'"

Name _____

Date _____

Response to Literature: Is *The Great Gatsby* Great?

Directions: *The Great Gatsby* is one of the most well-known and respected American novels. Some say is it the quintessential American novel. What do you think? Take a position and write a paper arguing for or against the enduring qualities of the novel and whether they effectively articulate American identity and the American Dream.

_____

_____

_____

_____

_____

_____

_____

_____

_____

_____

_____

_____

_____

_____

Name _____

Date _____

Response to Literature Rubric

Directions: Use this rubric to evaluate student responses.

	Exceptional Writing	Quality Writing	Developing Writing
Focus and Organization	☐ States a clear opinion and elaborates well. Engages the reader from the opening hook through the middle to the conclusion. Demonstrates clear understanding of the intended audience and purpose of the piece.	☐ Provides a clear and consistent opinion. Maintains a clear perspective and supports it through elaborating details. Makes the opinion clear in the opening hook and summarizes well in the conclusion.	☐ Provides an inconsistent point of view. Does not support the topic adequately or misses pertinent information. Provides lack of clarity in the beginning, middle, and conclusion.
Text Evidence	☐ Provides comprehensive and accurate support. Includes relevant and worthwhile text references.	☐ Provides limited support. Provides few supporting text references.	☐ Provides very limited support for the text. Provides no supporting text references.
Written Expression	☐ Uses descriptive and precise language with clarity and intention. Maintains a consistent voice and uses an appropriate tone that supports meaning. Uses multiple sentence types and transitions well between ideas.	☐ Uses a broad vocabulary. Maintains a consistent voice and supports a tone and feelings through language. Varies sentence length and word choices.	☐ Uses a limited and unvaried vocabulary. Provides an inconsistent or weak voice and tone. Provides little to no variation in sentence type and length.
Language Conventions	☐ Capitalizes, punctuates, and spells accurately. Demonstrates complete thoughts within sentences, with accurate subject-verb agreement. Uses paragraphs appropriately and with clear purpose.	☐ Capitalizes, punctuates, and spells accurately. Demonstrates complete thoughts within sentences and appropriate grammar. Paragraphs are properly divided and supported.	☐ Incorrectly capita... punctuates... Uses fra... sentence... Utilizes p... overall. Paragraphs... divided and...

The responses provided here are just examples of what the students may answer. Many accurate responses are possible for the questions throughout this unit.

During-Reading Vocabulary Activity—Section 1: Chapters 1–2 (page 16)

1. Daisy and Miss Baker appear to have been seated quite some time in the living room on the couch when Nick meets them. Neither is motivated to move much at all when he enters. Their conversation feels shallow and empty. Overall, each woman is excitable in moments, but neither says or does much of consequence.

2. Tom, described as a large, aggressive, and boastful character, seems to want to show off with Myrtle in front of Nick. He displays his wealth in buying the puppy for Myrtle, in keeping a separate apartment, and in throwing an impromptu party with lots of alcohol. He seems proud to be carrying on with two women at once. This makes him feel powerful and virile.

Close Reading the Literature—Section 1: Chapters 1–2 (page 21)

1. Through the voice of Nick, Fitzgerald describes a wasteland between West Egg and New York in his description of the valley of ashes. In direct contrast to the luscious interior description of the Buchanan home and the grandiose description of Gatsby's mansion, this area of land is "desolate," the men are "crumbling through the powdery air," and the eyes of Doctor T. J. Eckleburg "look out of no face."

2. Fitzgerald creates a lifeless and depressive mood in this passage, using such language as "grey land," "spasms of bleak dust," "eternal blindness," "small foul river,"and"a trail of ashes."

3. Nick already knows about Tom's mistress, Myrtle, from his conversation with Miss Baker. He claims he does not want to meet her, but admits he would like to see her from a distance. Nick seems like the kind of man who doesn't want to get too involved, preferring to keep his personal life simple and clean.

4. The eyes of Eckleburg give a portentous feel here early in the novel. There is an overbearing feeling of watchfulness. Note that it is in this scene and this infertile valley that the illicit affair between Tom and Myrtle is first displayed. The reader feels the tension building in the story.

During-Reading Vocabulary Activity—Section 2: Chapters 3–4 (page 26)

1. The partiers seem quite shallow and don't appear to have anything substantive to discuss. They fritter away their time drinking, dancing, and fighting. It makes sense that they would gossip about Gatsby, as they hardly know him. In fact, many have never even met him. People will make things up about others when they are trying to figure them out.

2. Jordan learns that Gatsby met Daisy long ago and has been in love with her ever since. He purchased the house in West Egg and throws the elaborate parties to get Daisy's attention and prove himself to her. He hopes that Jordan will help him meet up with Daisy once again.

Close Reading the Literature—Section 2: Chapters 3–4 (page 31)

1. Something about the way Gatsby makes the statement about being educated at Oxford seems off to Nick. He indicates that Gatsby "hurried the phrase" or "swallowed it, or choked on it." He feels that Gatsby does not seem fully comfortable making the statement, as if it bothers him to say it.

2. Gatsby's stories of international travel and adventure sound ludicrous to Nick. He finds himself picturing a young Gatsby as a "turbaned 'character'" who leaks "sawdust at every pore" and pursues tigers. Nick thinks that Gatsby's story so far is ridiculous.

3. To support his story, Gatsby shows Nick a war medal called an *Orderi di Danilo*, which he says was given to him by the country of Montenegro. He also shows Nick a photograph of himself with some friends standing in Trinity Quad at Oxford. Nick is astounded to be presented with actual evidence to support Gatsby's wild life story.

4. Gatsby informs Nick that later in the day, he plans to ask him for a favor. He says that, as he needs Nick's help, he doesn't want Nick to see him as "just some nobody." He worries that his tendency to drift around, "trying to forget the sad thing that happened to me" has made him hard to know and trust.

Close Reading the Literature—Section 3: Chapters 5–6 (page 41)

1. Gatsby acknowledges that the Buchanan home resides just on the other side of the water where the green light shines. The light has served as a beacon of desire and hope, a tenuous connection with his lost love. It helped him to hold onto his dream of a reunion with Daisy. This romantic admission touches Daisy, who puts "her arm through his abruptly."

2. Answers may vary. Some may assert that Nick's presence allows both Gatsby and Daisy to feel more comfortable because each of them have a personal, honest, and family-like relationship with Nick. Also, his company serves as a kind of buffer, allowing them to be more comfortable. Also, Nick is not of the upper class, so neither Gatsby nor Daisy stand on ceremony, risking typical upper-class judgment from him.

3. Gatsby receives a business call. He conducts a swift, cryptic conversation about a business associate who might not be working out. Gatsby gets off the phone quickly because he doesn't want to reveal too much about his specific financial dealings in front of Daisy. His business is mysterious, but the reader can tell that it isn't quite on the up and up.

4. Nick realizes that one's keen expectations are rarely met and usually disappoint, in fact. Additionally, memories often contain only the positive and do not really reflect reality. Gatsby has turned Daisy into such a perfect ideal in his memory that the real thing, no matter how beautiful and vibrant, can only pale in comparison.

During-Reading Vocabulary Activity—Section 4: Chapter 7 (page 46)

1. It is ironic that the "Wedding March" plays loudly in the ballroom below as Tom, Gatsby, and Daisy hash out their romantic triangle. The lack of sanctity in Tom and Daisy's marriage is apparent, as affairs by both are brought to light and openly discussed.

2. At this point in the novel, Nick realizes that Tom and Daisy do not have any real, private relationship with each other. They seem comfortable and even happy to invite witnesses to observe the deconstruction of their empty marriage. True to form, however, even when at their worst the couple remains convinced of their superiority. They find their own lives so compelling, they assume that others would be charmed to observe their emotional argument.

Close Reading the Literature—Section 4: Chapter 7 (page 51)

1. Gatsby is desperate to believe in the purity of the love between Daisy and him. He wants to believe that she could never truly love Tom and made an impulsive error in marrying him. He tries to make that true by saying it aloud.

2. Daisy first is angry and talks scornfully to Tom. Then, panic sets in as she realizes that things have progressed further than she ever planned. She throws a cigarette and lit match to the floor. She begins to "sob uncontrollably."

3. Tom says that once in a while he just "goes off on a spree" but he always comes back to Daisy.

4. Tom says the only way Gatsby could have met Daisy is by delivering groceries to her house. He calls him a "common swindler" who would have to steal a ring to marry Daisy. He makes allegations about Gatsby's business dealings.

Close Reading the Literature--Section 5: Chapters 8–9 (page 61)

1. Wilson begins to think about who might have been involved with his wife. He mentions the yellow car that hit her, and says he has ways of finding out to whom it belongs.

2. Hidden in a drawer, Wilson finds an expensive dog leash, made of leather and braided silver. To his knowledge, his wife does not have a dog. Additionally, he knows that Myrtle could not afford such a luxurious leash. The leash reveals to him that his wife has secrets.

3. Wilson decides that his wife was having an affair, and that she was murdered by her lover. He declares, "Then he killed her." and "He murdered her." He no longer thinks Myrtle's death was an accident.

4. The advertisement, which looms over Wilson's rear window, becomes a symbol of God for the man. He stares at it as he says, "You may fool me, but you can't fool God!" and "God sees everything." Wilson seems to be becoming unhinged, while also becoming obsessed with vengeance.

Comprehension Assessment (pages 67–68)

1. Nick comes from a privileged, moneyed background. Thus he may have grown up with certain expectations about social class and about how people are "supposed" to act. However, his father wanted him to take care to look outside of those expectations and realize that there are many kinds of people in the world. This may explain why Nick is a good narrator. Like Tom and Daisy, he has certain preconceptions about society. But, unlike the Buchanans, he makes an effort to look deeper and try to see beyond them. Therefore, Nick is able to observe disparate characters such as Tom, Gatsby, Myrtle, and Mr. Wolfsheim, and depict them without bias.

2. A. Nick disapproves of Gatsby's flamboyant lifestyle but cannot help but like him as a person. D. Nick comes from a prominent, well-to-do family in the Midwest.

3. F. Nick first thinks they are fascinating but later finds them reprehensible.

4. C. "They were careless people, Tom and Daisy—they smashed up things and creatures and then retreated back into their money . . . ."

5. F. The past love between Daisy and Gatsby cannot be recaptured.

6. Young Daisy is already jaded. She feels as if she has already done and seen everything, and no surprises or true joy remain in life. Additionally, Daisy takes her life of privilege and ease for granted. Others work and care for their children and don't have the luxury of worrying about how they will fill their days. But Daisy is like a spoiled child, wanting instant gratification and constant excitement, but not wanting to take any responsibility.

7. C. No matter how hard we try, we cannot ever truly escape our past.

8. E. "So we beat on, boats against the current, borne back ceaselessly into the past."

© Shell Education